It Started with Nails

by Karl Juergens
Illustrated by Tom Graham

PEARSON

Glenview, Illinois • Boston, Massachusetts • Chandler, Arizona
Upper Saddle River, New Jersey

Johannes wanted to be a carpenter. But he had no wood. He had no tools. He had only nails.

Where can I find the things I need? Johannes wondered. Then he remembered. The marketplace would have those things!

---

wonder: to ask yourself

2

In the marketplace, Johannes saw a merchant. "I have nails, but I need some wood," Johannes said.

The merchant said, "Fix my sign with your nails. Then you can have some wood."

Johannes fixed the sign and took some wood.

Johannes saw a merchant selling hammers.

"I have wood and nails," he told the merchant. Now I need a hammer."

"My roof is broken," the merchant said. "If you fix my roof, I will give you a hammer."

Johannes agreed to fix the roof. The merchant gave him a hammer. Johannes used the hammer, some nails, and some wood to fix the roof. The happy merchant also gave Johannes some safety gear.

---

gear: material used for an activity

Johannes continued to walk. He saw a merchant selling saws.

"I want to be a carpenter," Johannes told him. "I have nails and wood. I have a hammer and safety gear. Now I need a saw."

saws

"If you make a shelf for me," the merchant told Johannes, "I will give you a saw."

Johannes wore his safety gear while he cut some wood. He used his hammer and nails to build a shelf for the merchant.

The next day, Johannes took his nails, wood, hammer, safety gear, and saw to the marketplace. He built his own shop. When he was done, he made a sign that said: *Carpenter*.

"Now I am a carpenter!" he said.

---

shop: a small store